# CURSIVE WRITING
## *Words*

Ages:
4-6 years

This book belongs to

----------------------------------

MOONSTONE

| apple | angel | ant | aeroplane |
| apple | angel | ant | aeroplane |
| apple | angel | ant | aeroplane |
| apple | angel | ant | aeroplane |
| | | | |
| | | | |
| | | | |
| | | | |
| | | | |
| | | | |

| ball | banana | bat | bear |
|------|--------|-----|------|
| ball | banana | bat | bear |
| ball | banana | bat | bear |
| ball | banana | bat | bear |
|  |  |  |  |
|  |  |  |  |
|  |  |  |  |
|  |  |  |  |
|  |  |  |  |
|  |  |  |  |

| car | crayons | cat | cap |
|-----|---------|-----|-----|
| car | crayons | cat | cap |
| car | crayons | cat | cap |
| car | crayons | cat | cap |
| | | | |
| | | | |
| | | | |
| | | | |
| | | | |
| | | | |

| drum | dolphin | dog | duck |
|---|---|---|---|
| drum | dolphin | dog | duck |
| drum | dolphin | dog | duck |
| drum | dolphin | dog | duck |

| eraser | elephant | egg | earth |
|--------|----------|-----|-------|
| eraser | elephant | egg | earth |
| eraser | elephant | egg | earth |
| eraser | elephant | egg | earth |
|  |  |  |  |
|  |  |  |  |
|  |  |  |  |
|  |  |  |  |
|  |  |  |  |
|  |  |  |  |

| flower | football | fox | fish |
|--------|----------|-----|------|
| flower | football | fox | fish |
| flower | football | fox | fish |
| flower | football | fox | fish |
| | | | |
| | | | |
| | | | |
| | | | |
| | | | |
| | | | |

| grass | giraffe | girl | grapes |
|---|---|---|---|
| grass | giraffe | girl | grapes |
| grass | giraffe | girl | grapes |
| grass | giraffe | girl | grapes |
| | | | |
| | | | |
| | | | |
| | | | |
| | | | |
| | | | |

| horse | house | hen | hat |
|-------|-------|-----|-----|
| horse | house | hen | hat |
| horse | house | hen | hat |
| horse | house | hen | hat |

  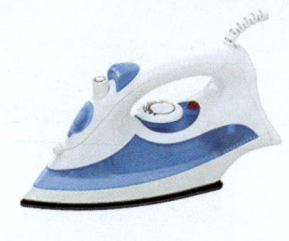 

| inkpot | iguana | iron | igloo |
|--------|--------|------|-------|
| inkpot | iguana | iron | igloo |
| inkpot | iguana | iron | igloo |
| inkpot | iguana | iron | igloo |
| | | | |
| | | | |
| | | | |
| | | | |
| | | | |
| | | | |

| jupiter | jacket | jug | jeep |
|---------|--------|-----|------|
| jupiter | jacket | jug | jeep |
| jupiter | jacket | jug | jeep |
| jupiter | jacket | jug | jeep |
|  |  |  |  |
|  |  |  |  |
|  |  |  |  |
|  |  |  |  |
|  |  |  |  |
|  |  |  |  |

   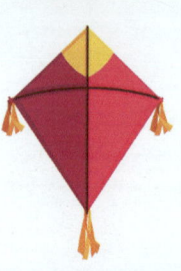

| king | kitten | key | kite |
|---|---|---|---|
| king | kitten | key | kite |
| king | kitten | key | kite |
| king | kitten | key | kite |
| | | | |
| | | | |
| | | | |
| | | | |
| | | | |
| | | | |

| lion | lotus | lamp | leaf |
|------|-------|------|------|
| lion | lotus | lamp | leaf |
| lion | lotus | lamp | leaf |
| lion | lotus | lamp | leaf |
|  |  |  |  |
|  |  |  |  |
|  |  |  |  |
|  |  |  |  |
|  |  |  |  |
|  |  |  |  |

| mango | monkey | map | moon |
|---|---|---|---|
| mango | monkey | map | moon |
| mango | monkey | map | moon |
| mango | monkey | map | moon |
| | | | |
| | | | |
| | | | |
| | | | |
| | | | |
| | | | |

| notebook | nut | nurse | nest |
|---|---|---|---|
| notebook | nut | nurse | nest |
| notebook | nut | nurse | nest |
| notebook | nut | nurse | nest |
| | | | |
| | | | |
| | | | |
| | | | |
| | | | |
| | | | |

| orchid | orange | ox | owl |
|--------|--------|-----|------|
| orchid | orange | ox | owl |
| orchid | orange | ox | owl |
| orchid | orange | ox | owl |
| | | | |
| | | | |
| | | | |
| | | | |
| | | | |
| | | | |

| pencil | parrot | pear | penguin |
|--------|--------|------|---------|
| pencil | parrot | pear | penguin |
| pencil | parrot | pear | penguin |
| pencil | parrot | pear | penguin |
| | | | |
| | | | |
| | | | |
| | | | |
| | | | |
| | | | |
| | | | |

| quail | queen | quilt | quill |
|-------|-------|-------|-------|
| quail | queen | quilt | quill |
| quail | queen | quilt | quill |
| quail | queen | quilt | quill |
|       |       |       |       |
|       |       |       |       |
|       |       |       |       |
|       |       |       |       |
|       |       |       |       |
|       |       |       |       |

| rabbit | ring | rainbow | rose |
|--------|------|---------|------|
| rabbit | ring | rainbow | rose |
| rabbit | ring | rainbow | rose |
| rabbit | ring | rainbow | rose |
|  |  |  |  |
|  |  |  |  |
|  |  |  |  |
|  |  |  |  |
|  |  |  |  |
|  |  |  |  |

| snake | sun | swan | ship |
|-------|-----|------|------|
| snake | sun | swan | ship |
| snake | sun | swan | ship |
| snake | sun | swan | ship |
| | | | |
| | | | |
| | | | |
| | | | |
| | | | |
| | | | |

| train | tiger | tortoise | teacher |
|-------|-------|----------|---------|
| train | tiger | tortoise | teacher |
| train | tiger | tortoise | teacher |
| train | tiger | tortoise | teacher |
| | | | |
| | | | |
| | | | |
| | | | |
| | | | |
| | | | |

| uniform | umbrella | urn | unicorn |
|---------|----------|-----|---------|
| uniform | umbrella | urn | unicorn |
| uniform | umbrella | urn | unicorn |
| uniform | umbrella | urn | unicorn |
|         |          |     |         |
|         |          |     |         |
|         |          |     |         |
|         |          |     |         |
|         |          |     |         |
|         |          |     |         |

| vulture | violin | van | vase |
|---------|--------|-----|------|
| vulture | violin | van | vase |
| vulture | violin | van | vase |
| vulture | violin | van | vase |
| | | | |
| | | | |
| | | | |
| | | | |
| | | | |

| watch | whale | wool | wolf |
|-------|-------|------|------|
| watch | whale | wool | wolf |
| watch | whale | wool | wolf |
| watch | whale | wool | wolf |
| | | | |
| | | | |
| | | | |
| | | | |
| | | | |
| | | | |

  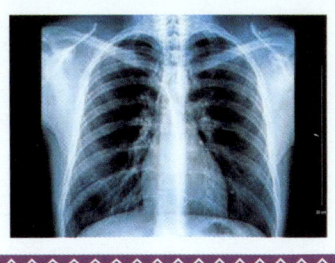 

| xerus | xylophone | x-ray | xenops |
|---|---|---|---|
| xerus | xylophone | x-ray | xenops |
| xerus | xylophone | x-ray | xenops |
| xerus | xylophone | x-ray | xenops |
| | | | |
| | | | |
| | | | |
| | | | |
| | | | |
| | | | |

 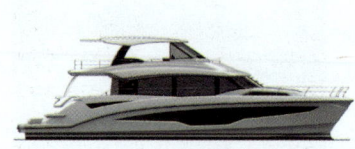  

| yoga | yacht | yak | yellow |
|------|-------|-----|--------|
| yoga | yacht | yak | yellow |
| yoga | yacht | yak | yellow |
| yoga | yacht | yak | yellow |
| | | | |
| | | | |
| | | | |
| | | | |
| | | | |
| | | | |

| zero | zebra | zipper | zoo |
|------|-------|--------|-----|
| zero | zebra | zipper | zoo |
| zero | zebra | zipper | zoo |
| zero | zebra | zipper | zoo |
|  |  |  |  |
|  |  |  |  |
|  |  |  |  |
|  |  |  |  |
|  |  |  |  |
|  |  |  |  |

# REVISION TIME

| crab | dinosaur | alligator | bicycle |
|------|----------|-----------|---------|
| crab | dinosaur | alligator | bicycle |
| crab | dinosaur | alligator | bicycle |
| crab | dinosaur | alligator | bicycle |
|      |          |           |         |
|      |          |           |         |
|      |          |           |         |
|      |          |           |         |
|      |          |           |         |
|      |          |           |         |

# REVISION TIME

| goose | helicopter | eggplant | frog |
|-------|------------|----------|------|
| goose | helicopter | eggplant | frog |
| goose | helicopter | eggplant | frog |
| goose | helicopter | eggplant | frog |
| | | | |
| | | | |
| | | | |
| | | | |
| | | | |
| | | | |

# REVISION TIME

| koala | ladybug | island | jaguar |
|-------|---------|--------|--------|
| koala | ladybug | island | jaguar |
| koala | ladybug | island | jaguar |
| koala | ladybug | island | jaguar |
|       |         |        |        |
|       |         |        |        |
|       |         |        |        |
|       |         |        |        |
|       |         |        |        |
|       |         |        |        |

# REVISION TIME

| octopus | pineapple | mountain | newspaper |
|---------|-----------|----------|-----------|
| octopus | pineapple | mountain | newspaper |
| octopus | pineapple | mountain | newspaper |
| octopus | pineapple | mountain | newspaper |
|  |  |  |  |
|  |  |  |  |
|  |  |  |  |
|  |  |  |  |
|  |  |  |  |
|  |  |  |  |

# CAN YOU FORM WORDS WITH EACH VOWEL?

| a | e | i | o | u |
|---|---|---|---|---|
|   |   |   |   |   |
|   |   |   |   |   |
|   |   |   |   |   |
|   |   |   |   |   |
|   |   |   |   |   |
|   |   |   |   |   |
|   |   |   |   |   |
|   |   |   |   |   |
|   |   |   |   |   |